A Guide to Revolting Rome

Mick Gowar

OXFORD
UNIVERSITY PRESS

OXFORD
UNIVERSITY PRESS

is a department of the University of Oxford.
It furthers the University's objective of excellence in research, scholarship,
and education by publishing worldwide in

Oxford New York
Auckland Cape Town Dar es Salaam Hong Kong Karachi
Kuala Lumpur Madrid Melbourne Mexico City Nairobi
New Delhi Shanghai Taipei Toronto

With offices in

Argentina Austria Brazil Chile Czech Republic France Greece
Guatemala Hungary Italy Japan Poland Portugal Singapore
South Korea Switzerland Thailand Turkey Ukraine Vietnam

First published 2007

British Library Cataloguing in Publication Data

Data available

ISBN: 978-0-19-846112-8

5 7 9 10 8 6 4

Printed in China

Paper used in the production of this book is a natural,
recyclable product made from wood grown in sustainable forests.
The manufacturing process conforms to the environmental
regulations of the country of origin

Acknowledgements

The publisher would like to thank the following for permission to reproduce photographs: p10
Peter Connolly/AKG – Images; p14 David W. Hamilton/Alamy; p21 Museo Civico @1990/Photo Scala,
Florence; p23 The Trustees of the British Museum

Illustrations by Martin Aston

Contents

A Grumpy Old Roman

We'll visit the baths.
It's so noisy you're sure to get a headache!
I'll take you to watch wealthy Romans eating at a feast.
That'll make you feel sick!
I'll tell you about the nasty things that Roman doctors and priests do.
I hope you've got a strong stomach!
I'll tell you about our Emperor.
But be careful – being rude about the Emperor can be dangerous!

Bad Buildings
The first thing I want to show you is how we Romans really live. You may have seen pictures of Roman villas and palaces. You probably think all Romans live in buildings like that. We don't.
Most Romans live in small flats in big blocks like this one.
There are shops on the ground floor and two, three or even four floors of flats above. Sometimes six people share one tiny flat.
The rich men who own these blocks of flats are only interested in making as much money as they can. They don't look after the buildings. Every week people are killed when the buildings fall down or catch fire.

It made me so angry that I wrote this:
We live in a city held up by bits of wood for that is how the landlord holds up his falling-down house. He patches up gaping cracks in the old wall. He tells the people not to worry and to go to sleep under a roof ready to fall on their heads!

The Great Fire of Rome

And with all the badly built buildings and crowded streets there are lots of fires.
The worst fire was in the Year 64 when Nero was Emperor. That fire destroyed nearly three quarters of Rome.
Nero came rushing back from his holiday home as soon as he heard about the fire. He even tried to organise fire-fighters.
But lots of people in Rome believe Nero started the fire himself. Some people say they saw him playing his lyre and singing when the fire was at its worst. He looked as if he was happy that Rome was burning!

'Bread and Circuses'

We have more than 150 holidays a year. On most holidays the Emperor pays for free gladiator shows at the Colosseum.
Many Romans go to the Colosseum as they really enjoy watching gladiators fighting – to the death, sometimes.

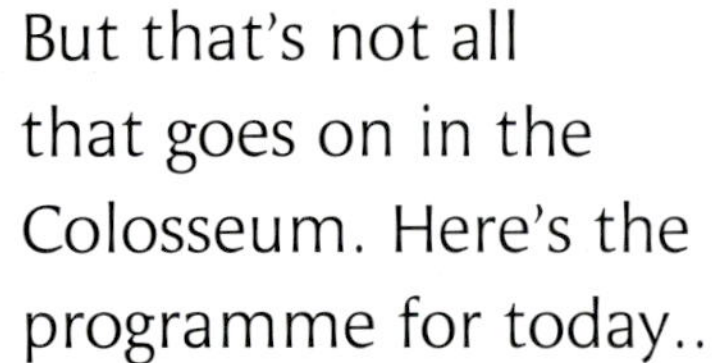

But that's not all that goes on in the Colosseum. Here's the programme for today...

Morning

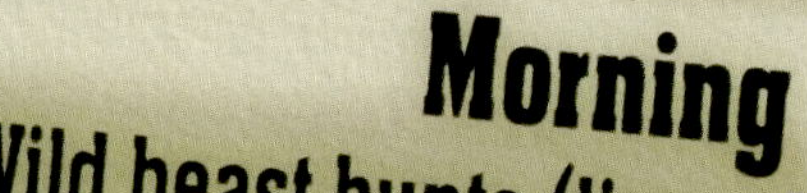

Wild beast hunts (lions, hippos, bears hunted and killed)

Lunchtime

Criminals punished by being killed and eaten by wild animals

Afternoon

Gladiator fights

The shows in the Colosseum make me angry. All anybody cares about these days is getting free food and free shows.

On the first day that the Colosseum was opened, 5,000 wild animals and 4,000 tame animals were killed! I don't like seeing criminals being killed by lions and bears either.

Work

All our houses, temples and shops are built by slaves.

All our pots and plates are made by slaves.

It's slaves who work in the mines and on our farms.

Most of our doctors, teachers, clerks and artists are slaves, too.

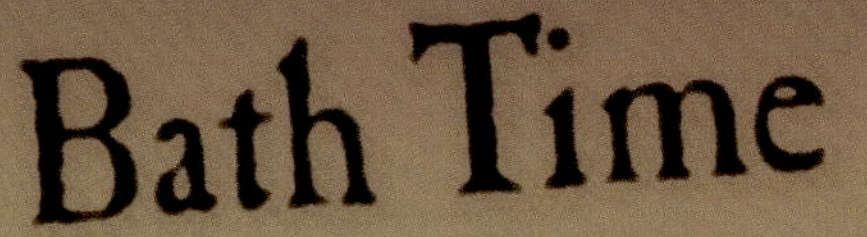

Bath Time

After seeing a show most Romans like to go to the baths. Our baths are like your saunas. We Romans don't use soap, we rub ourselves with oil instead.

We sweat until all the dirt comes to the surface, then a slave scrapes all the dirt and oil off with a blunt knife called a strigil. What a horrible job!

A writer I know called Seneca lived in a flat over a bath house. He hated it. This is why:

I can't stand the noise! The strong men groaning when they swing the heavy weights.

The slap of the masseur's hand, pummelling some chap's shoulders.

Do your teeth need whitening?
Try these Roman remedies:
❖ dried powdered mouse brains
or
❖ dogs teeth burnt and the ashes ground up and mixed with honey.

And the fellow who loves to hear his own voice in the bath – what a racket!
And the only time the barber stops chattering is when he's plucking armpits and making his customers yell!

Going to a Feast

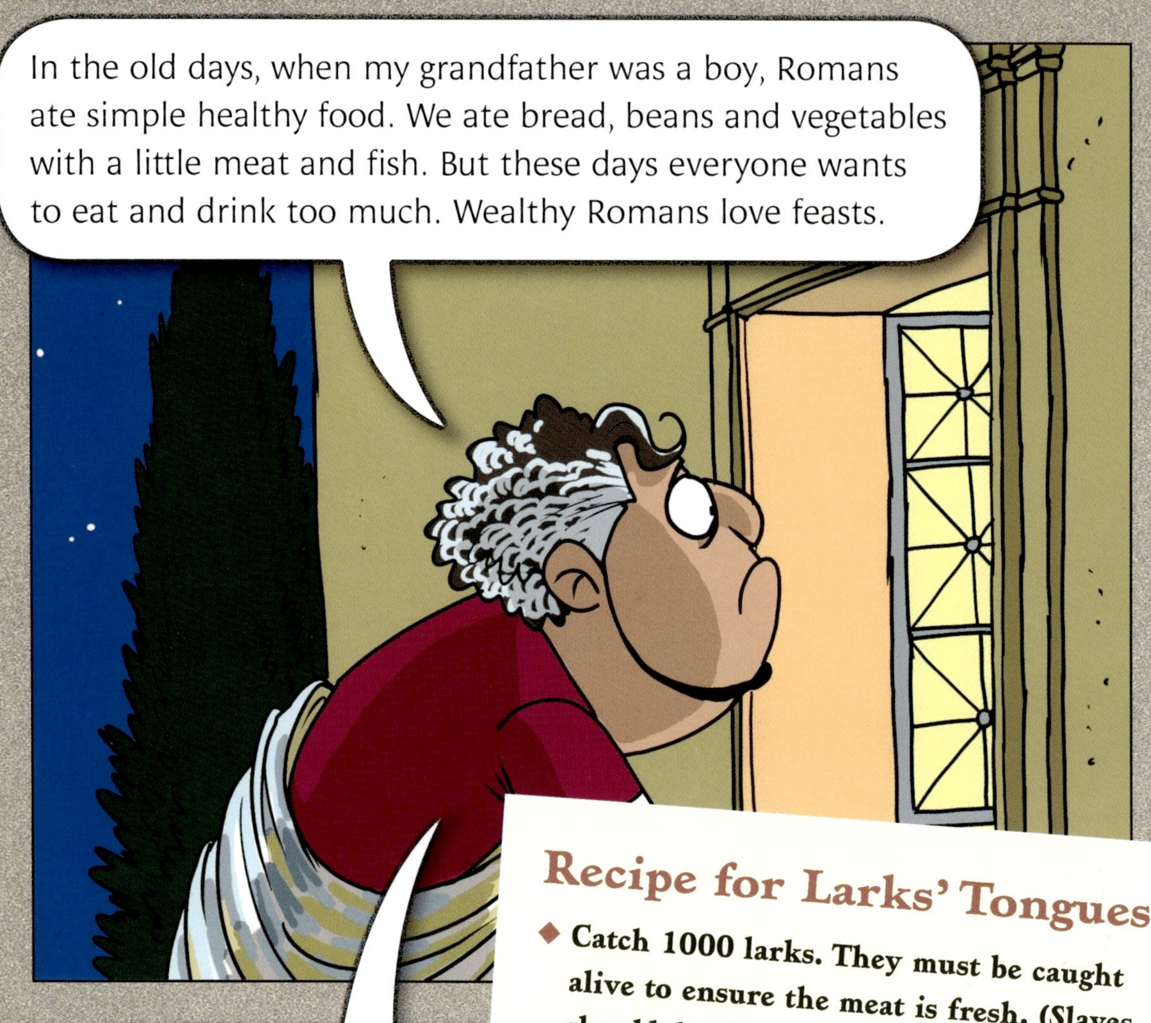

Some people like to show how rich they are by making up silly dishes which are very expensive. Look at this recipe:

Recipe for Larks' Tongues

- Catch 1000 larks. They must be caught alive to ensure the meat is fresh. (Slaves should do this.)
- The day before your feast kill the birds.
- Open the beaks.
- Cut out the tongues.
- Soak in red wine overnight.
- Strain off the wine and serve to your guests.

I once went to a feast where the first course was stuffed dormice!
Some wealthy Romans are so greedy they make themselves sick half way through a meal so they can keep on eating!

Feeling Poorly?

Rome isn't a good place to be ill. There are lots of doctors, but most of them are useless. Frauds – that's what I call them. All they do is look at your horoscope and give you medicine that doesn't work – or makes you feel much worse! And they charge a fortune.

This is what my friend Martial wrote about his doctor:

I felt a little ill and called
Dr Symmachus.
Well, you came, Symmachus,
but you brought 100 medical
students with you.
One hundred ice-cold hands
poked and jabbed me.
I didn't have a fever,
Symmachus, when I called
you – but now I do!

Army doctors are very good at healing wounds. They can stitch cuts and mend broken bones, just like your doctors. They even use plasters to stop bleeding. Our plasters are made from spiders webs mixed with honey – but they work.
But if you've got a cold or fever or stomach ache, don't call for a doctor. He'll only make you worse!

Gods and Goddesses

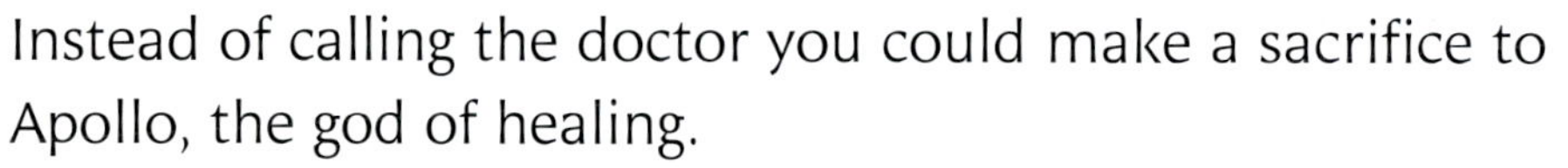

Instead of calling the doctor you could make a sacrifice to Apollo, the god of healing.

We Romans have many gods and goddesses. We try to keep the gods and goddesses happy by giving them animal sacrifices.

We believe that the gods and goddesses speak to us in a sort of code. We believe they send us messages in the livers of the animals we sacrifice.

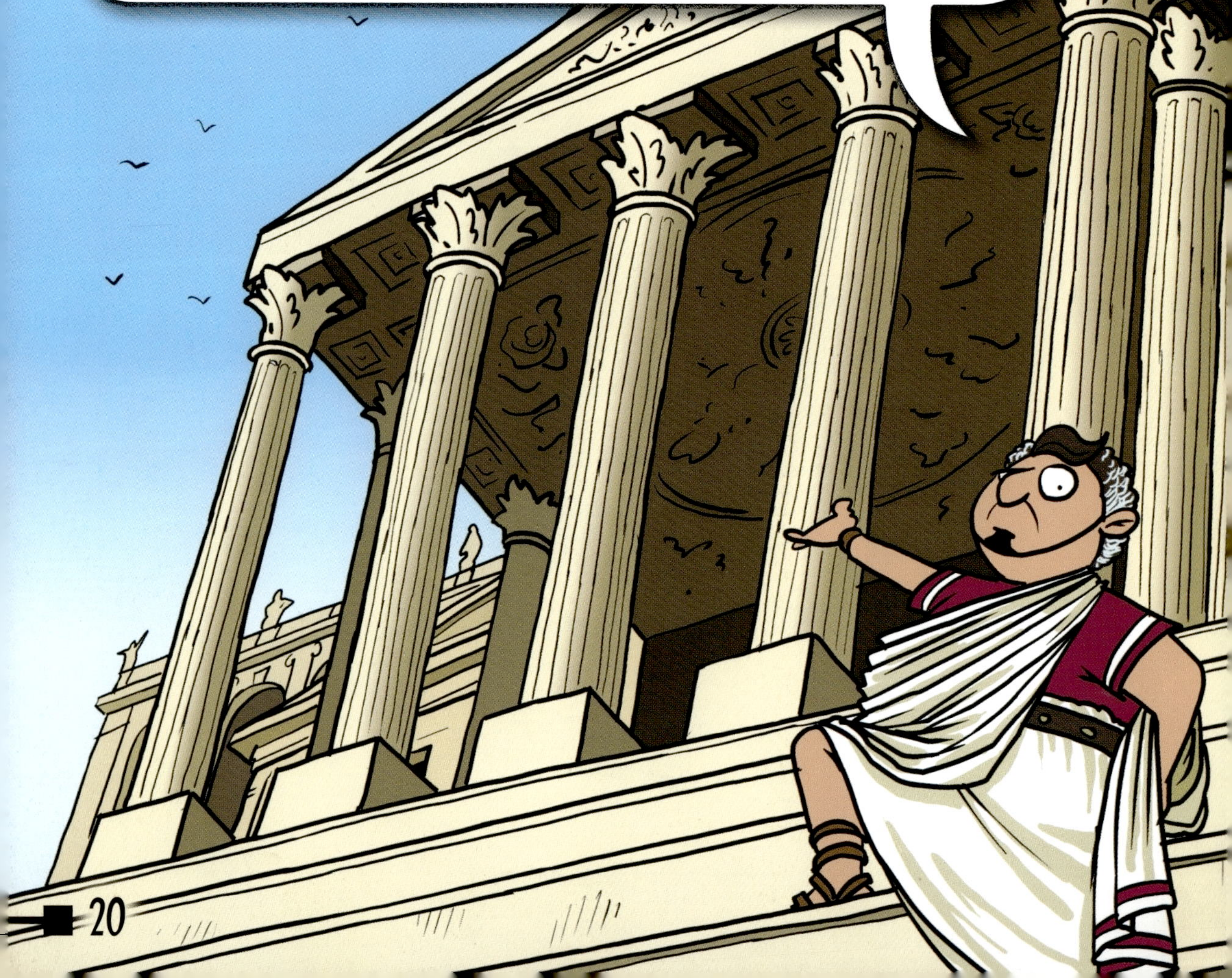

After the animal has been sacrificed, a priest called a Haruspex looks at its liver and can tell:

- whether the god or goddess is happy or angry
- if it's a good day to get married
- if it's a good day to borrow money
- whether someone's stomach ache or headache will get better.

This is a bronze model of a liver. It's used to teach young priests which part of the liver gives the different messages!

The Divine Emperor

At the beginning of his reign, Domitian would spend hours alone every day doing nothing but catching flies and stabbing them with a needle-sharp pen.

He was even cruel to insects. Seutonius, an author, wrote this about Domitian:

When I wrote a poem against him, he banished me to Egypt. I had no money and had to beg for food.

Hadrian is our emperor now. He is a fair man and a brave soldier. But will our next emperor be a madman like Nero or Domitian? I dread to think what will happen to Rome if he is!

Famous Romans

Augustus

Emperor from 27 BC – AD 14
The first Roman emperor.

Nero

Emperor from AD 54–68 believed he was a wonderful poet and singer but was neither. He entered many singing and acting competitions which he always won – but only because he was the emperor!

Domitian

Emperor from AD 81 – 96
Famous for his cruelty, especially to Christians and Jews who he had killed in large numbers in the Colosseum and other arenas.

Hadrian

Emperor from AD 117–138
Emperor and soldier who visited England to supervise the building of Hadrian's wall – the great wall stretching across the north of England.

Martial

Roman writer (probably between AD 86 and 103)
Friend of Juvenal. He wrote many epigrams – very short poems – a lot of them making fun of the Romans he disliked.

Juvenal

Roman writer (probably between AD 100 and 128)
Best known for his 16 Satires – poems complaining about life in ancient Rome.